DRAGONFLIES

NICOLE HELGET

Published by Creative Education

P.O. Box 227, Mankato, Minnesota 56002

Creative Education is an imprint of The Creative Company

Design and production by Stephanie Blumenthal

Printed in the United States of America

Photographs by Blair Nikula, Entomological Society of America / Ries Memorial Slide
Collection, Getty Images (Aurora Outdoor Collection / Peter Dennen,
Bruce Coleman, Darlyne A. Murawski, Photographer's Choice, Taxi / Larry West)

Library of Congress Cataloging-in-Publication Data

Helget, Nicole Lea, 1976–

Dragonflies / by Nicole Helget.

p. cm. — (BugBooks)

Includes index.

ISBN-13: 978-1-58341-541-2

1. Dragonflies—Juvenile literature. I. Title.

QL520.H45 2007

595.7'33—DC22   2006018238

24689753

DUCK! HERE COMES A RED ONE. THERE GOES A BLUE ONE! THEY DIP, DIVE, AND WHIZ THROUGH THE AIR. SHINY WINGS CARRY LONG, LIGHT BODIES. DRAGONFLIES ARE ON THE HUNT FOR FOOD!

DRAGONFLIES ARE INSECTS.
THEY ARE CALLED DRAGONFLIES BE-

CAUSE THEY LOOK LIKE DRAGONS IN FAIRY TALES. THEY HAVE BIG EYES AND A LARGE JAW. THEY HAVE WINGS AND A LONG TAIL.

Dragonflies come in many sizes and colors.

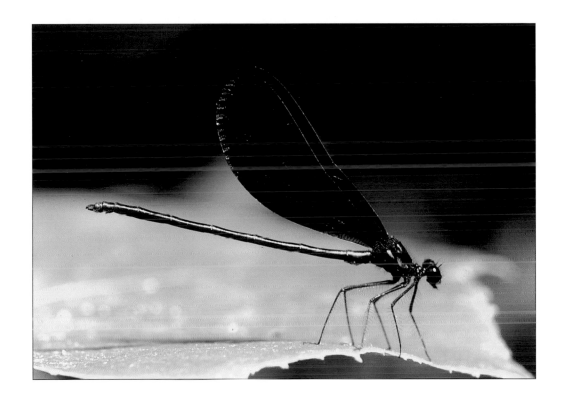

DRAGONFLY WINGS A dragonfly can fly 30 miles (48 km) per hour. That makes it one of the fastest insects in the world! Dragonfly wings are usually see-through, but some are colorful.

A DRAGONFLY HAS TWO ANTEN-
NAE (AN-*TEN*-NAY) AND TWO BIG
EYES. ITS EYES ARE
PERFECT FOR HUNT-
ING OTHER INSECTS
SUCH AS MOSQUI-
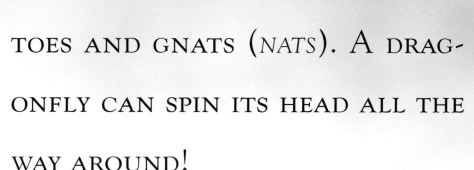
TOES AND GNATS (*NATS*). A DRAG-
ONFLY CAN SPIN ITS HEAD ALL THE
WAY AROUND!

A dragonfly's eyes take up most of its head.

A DRAGONFLY HAS FOUR WINGS AND SIX LEGS. A DRAGONFLY'S LONG WINGS FLAP VERY QUICKLY. ITS LEGS ARE TOO WEAK FOR WALKING.

A DRAGON-FLY USES ITS LEGS TO HOLD FOOD WHILE IT FLIES THROUGH THE AIR.

Dragonfly wings are thin but strong.

NEEDLE BUG *Some people call the dragonfly the "devil's darning needle." That is because a dragonfly's long body looks like a needle. But dragonflies are not sharp and cannot sting.*

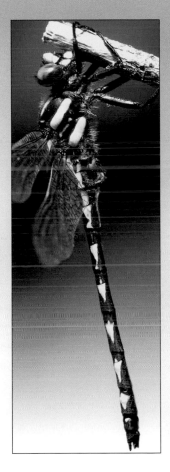

A DRAGONFLY'S BELLY IS LONG AND THIN. IT IS ALSO COLORFUL. SOME DRAGONFLIES ARE RED, GREEN, OR PURPLE. OTHERS ARE YELLOW OR BLUE.

Some dragonflies have spots or stripes.

MOST DRAGONFLIES BEGIN LIFE IN WATER OR CLOSE TO WATER. FE-MALE DRAGONFLIES LAY EGGS ON  PLANTS OR RIGHT ON THE WATER. MALE DRAGONFLIES CHASE AWAY PREDATORS SUCH AS OTHER INSECTS AND BIRDS.

Some dragonflies lay eggs on plants.

  13

NYMPH LIPS *The dragonfly nymph is a big eater. When it sees food, the nymph shoots out its long lip. The lip grabs the food and pulls it into the nymph's mouth.*

A BABY DRAGONFLY IS CALLED A
"NYMPH" (*NIMF*). IT IS ALWAYS HUNGRY.

IT FINDS FOOD IN
OR AROUND THE
WATER. A NYMPH
EATS INSECTS, BABY FROGS, AND
EVEN OTHER NYMPHS. THE NYMPH
SOON GROWS TOO BIG FOR ITS SKIN.

Nymphs eat many things—even small fish.

THE NYMPH SHEDS ITS OLD SKIN.
IT GROWS EVEN BIGGER. AFTER ONE

OR TWO YEARS,
THE NYMPH STOPS
GROWING. IT IS
NOW AN ADULT
DRAGONFLY. IT STRETCHES ITS WINGS
AND FLIES FOR THE FIRST TIME.

Nymphs shed their skin when they become adults.

SOMETIMES, DRAGONFLY NYMPHS

EAT TOO MANY BABY FISH IN PONDS

 AND LAKES. SOME

DRAGONFLIES EAT TOO

MANY HONEYBEES. BUT

DRAGONFLIES ARE USU-

ALLY HELPFUL TO HUMANS. THEY

EAT BUGS THAT BITE PEOPLE.

Dragonflies eat mosquitoes. Spiders eat dragonflies.

HUNTER AND HUNTED

Dragonflies are good hunters. But some creatures hunt dragonflies. Birds, frogs, and spiders all eat dragonflies. Some fish snatch female dragonflies as they lay their eggs.

DRAGONFLIES ARE PRETTY TO LOOK AT. NEXT TIME YOU TAKE A WALK, SEE HOW MANY DIFFERENT DRAGONFLIES YOU CAN FIND!

Dragonflies' colorful bodies are easy to spot.

GLOSSARY

ANTENNAE — THE TWO LONG RODS ON TOP OF A DRAGON-

FLY'S HEAD

INSECTS — BUGS THAT HAVE SIX LEGS

PREDATORS — ANIMALS THAT KILL AND EAT OTHER ANIMALS

SHEDS — LOSES SKIN

  23

INDEX

ANIMALS 12, 15, 18, 19

ANTENNAE 6, 23

COLOR 3, 5, 11, 20

EGGS 12, 19

EYES 4, 6

INSECTS 4, 6, 12, 15, 23

JAWS 4

LEGS 8

NYMPHS 14, 15, 16, 18

PREDATORS 12, 23

SHEDDING 16, 23

WINGS 3, 4, 5, 8, 16